Braided Words,
Braided Lives

Braided Words, Braided Lives

Poetry by members of
Prince Chapel African Methodist Episcopal Church
and
Saint Mark's Presbyterian Church
of Tucson, Arizona

Edited by Oletha Bostic Gustus

Committee Members

Gladys Ahmad, Prince Chapel African Methodist Episcopal Church
Oletha Bostic Gustus, Saint Mark's Presbyterian Church
Jeanette J. Jones, Saint Mark's Presbyterian Church
Charlene Jones Metoyer, Prince Chapel African Methodist Episcopal Church
Jessie Reasor Zander, Saint Mark's Presbyterian Church

Braided Words, Braided Lives

Published by Hats Off Books™
610 East Delano Street, Suite 104, Tucson, Arizona 85705 U.S.A.
www.hatsoffbooks.com

International Standard Book Number: 1-58736-311-9
Library of Congress Control Number: 2004101256

Cover Design: Gwyneth Roske, Saint Mark's Presbyterian Church

INTRODUCTION

In the year 2000, Saint Mark's Presbyterian Church undertook a joint project of building a Habitat for Humanity house with Prince Chapel African Methodist Episcopal Church. In the course of planning for this project, I frequently met for lunch with my counterpart from Prince Chapel, Gladys Ahmad. As we talked about our lives, we found so many things that we had in common—both of us had just retired from long teaching careers, both of us had an abiding faith and were involved on several committees in our churches, and both of us wrote poetry as a way of expressing ourselves. We spoke of this coincidence and of others we knew in our churches who wrote poetry. The idea for a book of poetry emerged and we promised to put a book together "once things settled down."

The "settling down" happened slowly, but eventually a committee was formed and poetry began to come in from our members. Members asked if they could include work of children and grandchildren who lived away and were not members and the circle was increased to include these poems that were dear to them. Many "closet poets" appeared who had been too shy to share their work before, and as we read these works of thoughts on the depth of our faith, our love of family, our respect for nature, our concern for the conditions of the world, and our ability to see the humor in everyday life, the title *Braided Words, Braided Lives* emerged.

As you read these poems, you are encouraged to read the biographies of the people who wrote them. Our contributors vary in age from nine years to over eighty; in education from those who have not finished high school to those with doctorates; and in experience from those limited by circumstance to those with unlimited opportunity. But their words are to be valued, because they are *their words*. Contributor Russell Long states, "I believe poetry moves through the brain to the pen as a gift that needs little or no revision." Writing is truly a gift, and through our writing we offer this gift to our congregations, our families, and to all who would be open to our words.

Oletha Bostic Gustus

Braided Words, Braided Lives

INSPIRED

by Gladys M. Ahmad

Awakening in the morning
with a freshness that
was not felt yesterday. Just
thinking of the wonderful
things that will be
encountered during this
new day. It comes from
being inspired by the
inner source that really
comes from on high!

"I"   Involved
"N"   Necessary
"S"   Spiritual
"P"   Prepared
"I"   Integrity
"R"   Richness
"E"   Energized
"D"   Dutiful

REALITY

by Gladys M. Ahmad

You can't have that which is not yours to be.
Understand that there are some things on display
and they are just for you to see.

But look around, at least
observe, lift your fantasy. Only
as a reminder: You must return
to Reality.

Let the inner feelings
grow. It is there where all
changes must take place,
and give you that extra
strength to go on and on.

Then, that which
is not yours, you no longer
want. There is no need to worry,
you have reached *REALITY*!!

RESPONDING

by Gladys M. Ahmad

I find myself thinking about
All the love that I am surrounded by
Realizing that I know it is love.

Because I love.

I love the people I know.
I love the beauty in the places to which I go.

I love the trees and mountains too.
In fact, I love all of the beauty
God has permitted me to feel and see.

Yes, when I find myself thinking about
All the love I feel and know

I am responding.

THE WORLD OF FRIENDS

by Rachel Campbell

I am dreaming
Love, laughter and peace are all around
Friends talk, laugh and sing, chatter
As time passes.
In this world friends are with everyone
The sun and the moon and midnight and noon
There is nothing wrong, no hurtful words, no loneliness
No mistakes that put you so low, oh so low...
Everyone is spunky, rosy and red
They are true to you—only you
Out of nowhere, the luminescent laughter is murdered
And you sit all alone—all alone
A mistake rakes away the leaves of your soul
Regrets are like shadows, haunting you everywhere
All good drains out like an old faucet
Slow, slow, slow...
You regret making the mistake that is making you ache
Like a knife slicing your heart
The one who hugged you now pushes you down
Where are you going?
You know they hurt themselves when you scream
"What did I do?"
But they're gone, out of the blue
What we call friendship dies like a plague, an epidemic, a mad rage
People can be cruel
They rip out souls like they were weeds on earth
They throw it down, stamp, stamp, stamp
Then they vanish
Friends can last a lifetime and that is what we want
Sometimes you suffer in order to get what you want
The lifelong goal is to stay close
But sometimes your dreams are hit like a baseball

They fly away
Out of the stadium
Until one lucky person
Picks up the ball and starts over again
Friends come
And go
But true ones live in your soul
Forever, forever more.

SEA GREEN

by Rachel Campbell

I dream a lullaby,
A fantasy
About the twilight
Of a glimmering sea.
The waves sweep against the sand
And the cold water tickles my tan.
I lie between the world
And the sea
And watch aquamarine water trickle beside me.
The twinkle of the evening stars
Shines light on the ocean floor
Forevermore.
The water in the twilight becomes a pool of life.
Then in the sunrise
The breeze is cool as the morning mist.
Optimism, peace, and solitude—
The sapphire water is contentment for me.
Look through your eyes
And see the glowing gifts
Of the tranquil sea.

STRANGER IN MY MIRROR

by Lou Carter

Who is that old one in my mirror there,
Some distant kin?
Or some old friend long since dead?
All that mess of gray hair
that never was supposed to be
anything but red.

What happened to that old skin
that used to be so pink and bright
now sagging and so white?

So I look again at that reflection
and I'm shocked to see
that stranger there
is me.

HELLO, DEATH

by Lou Carter

'Tho we've never met
I've known you.
I saw you in the stone-still faces
of father, mother, sister, brother
when they thought it best
to go with you
to eternal rest.

I knew you too that night
You knocked upon my door
My welcome guest
The night I fell on concrete floor.
I could have gone with you then
But I would not let you in.

There is more here than this old bag of bones I carry.
Joy, love, laughter,
words to write and say,
what I've done and where I've been
until today.
So I'll wait for God to say where and when
And I will go with you then, but not before.

COWARD

by Lou Carter

Coward, come and walk with me,
a coward too,
Who even fears what fear itself can do.
For we must learn that fear is but a challenge
to destinies unknown
and may be overcome with truth
When faith is shown.

So take my hand and walk a little way with me,
For with combined courage we may see,
That two may dispel the fear that one would know,
And together a stronger faith for both
May grow.

I AM A STRONG BLACK CHILD OF GOD

by Laona J. Crutcher

I am the strong Black child of God,
Full of grace and dignity.
And why?
Because my identity is in Jesus Christ.
He gives it to me.

I am a strong Black child of God my King,
And I am bold
For within me lives the Christ of
Pure, pure gold.

I am a strong Black child,
Not afraid of life here.
I will fight to study, to learn and
To be a winner.
I will be an example for Christ who died
So that I would not have to die a sinner.

He loves me, He protects me
He guides me, He gives me the ability
So that as a strong Black child of God
I can, and I will, live victoriously.

Freely, as a strong Black child
I have given Jesus full control of my life
And in doing so lose self and strife,
He is the way, the Truth and the Life, (John 3:16)
Jehovah Jireh—the Lord will provide. (Genesis 22:14)

LOVE—A WOVEN HEART

by Leticia Fagg

Some people ooze Love,
It flows freely.

Some people store Love,
It warms their hearts.

Some people avoid Love,
They're scared to try it.

Some people seek Love,
Their hearts are craving.

Some people never feel Love,
Their hearts are empty.

Think of each thread in your woven heart,
Contributed by each one you Love.

How are the strands of your heart woven?
Tautly strung?
Loosely hanging?
Uniform thickness?
Multicolored?
Evenly spaced?
Intertwined?
Segregated?
Hidden from view?
Pattern forming?

Keep building your woven heart,
Layer upon layer,
Until your heart is bursting,
Overflowing,
Warming the lives around you.

IF YOU WERE A TREE

by Leticia Fagg

Pretend you are a tree.

What kind of a tree would you like to be?
How did you start off in life?
Were you planted or cared for,
or did you blow in and have to learn to survive?

Are you deciduous,
with a life cycle with many highs and lows?
Or are you an evergreen,
fairly constant with steady changes and growth?

Are you shallow rooted,
finding your nourishment just below the surface?
Or are you deeply rooted,
searching deep, deep down?

Are you tall,
reaching up?
Or are you broad,
spreading yourself out?

Do you have a long trunk,
taking a long time to find your mission in life?
Or do you have a stubby trunk,
established quickly, ready to branch out at a young age?

Is your bark rough,
has life been hard for you?
Or is your bark smooth,
being blessed with an easy run?

Are your branches thick,
with you firmly set in your ways?
Or are your branches thin,
making you flexible and changeable?

Do you have any holes or nests?
Do you welcome guests into your home?
Do you like to keep to yourself?

Are you broad-leafed or spiky-leafed?
Are your flowers simple or intricate?
Are your fruits edible or not?

Have you ever been pruned,
or have you been allowed to grow on?
Have you suffered from flood or drought?

How many rings do you have?
Have you had many years to build wisdom,
or is wisdom still in its infancy?

What season of life are you presently in?
Are you bearing fruit?
Are you loosing leaves?
Are you growing buds?
Are you blossoming with flowers?

Whatever kind of tree you are
GOD LOVES YOU!
And he has a purpose for you.

Now keep your eyes closed and think about:
Your roots... Your trunk... Your branches...
Your leaves... Your flowers... and your fruit.

1998

*Written after doing a study on the Celtic Cross and
performed to flute music with creative movement.*

EASTER MORNING

by Leticia Fagg

Easter morning has come—
Open the curtain—Unveil the scene.

Breathe in the freshness of what you see,
Continue your journey,
Don't be laden down with Christ's heavy cross,
Take on the colours of God's world.
Set the world aglow with God's light,
Be one with God's creation.
Don't set yourself apart,
Follow your destiny,
Carry on:
    Seeking and searching,
        Nurturing and growing,
            Retracing and replotting.

Suck in the nourishment you need,
Grow and bear fruit,
And you will return from whence you came.

    From the soil we came—
        To the soil we go.

CHRISTIAN WOMEN REACHING HIGHER HEIGHTS

by Brenda Fleming

From the womb, brings forth woman
From the price Jesus paid, brings forth the Christian woman
Today the Christian woman, a rarity of
Competence
Strength
And Commitment
The Christian woman today, climbing higher heights,
Reaching a higher elevation of God's plateau
A woman of God
A woman born from the rib of man
Today we bring love, an agape love
Today we bring love, reflecting inner strength
Of
Self control
Self indulgence
And Self sacrificing
We are Christian women standing on God's promises
Christian women pruning for God's paradise
Christian women of an utmost God
We are Christian women reaching higher heights
Christian Women
We are.

October 2001

UNITY

by Brenda Fleming

Unity
the Black American experience
Unity
it set us free
Unity
does not have to mean
a melee but,
Unity
the Black American people
Unity
the Black woman
brought out of the pits of hell to embrace a
loveless America
Unity
the Black man. A statue of strength,
Love and Respect
The Black man embraces the
Black woman
Unity
The Black child, a
mind of determination and
tolerance The Black Child,
discipline and Respect with a vision
Unity
are we
Unity, we survived
Unity, is where we ought to be
Unity, is love for me.

JUST WHO I AM

by Brenda Fleming

And to me they say, "Who do you think you are?"
"We don't understand you."

Who I am, A Strong Black Woman
A Goddess of Survival
A legend of envy for my Strength

Who I am, A Strong Black Woman
A God fearing Woman
A Woman of Pride and Great Demeanor

Who I am, A Strong Black Woman
Whom many of my Caucasian brothers and sisters have
refused to accept because of my undying Strength
A Strong Black Woman, whom so many have envied my
desire and will to Survive the Stream of hurdles that are
Placed before me

Who I am, A Strong Black Woman
A Strong Black Woman that breathes Hope

Just Who I am,
A Strong Black Woman
Who is a Child of the King
and for this they don't understand

October 1994

WOMEN OF THE CHURCH

by Eugene L. Gable

The mixture of their sweet perfume
In church on Sunday day
The blending of their voices to sing
Was heard from far away.

Whose tears were quick to run in streams,
At what the preacher said
Released the burdens of their hearts
And let their souls be glad.

Who felt the need for tender hands
With strength beyond compare
To guide their children on the path
And lead them from despair.

And were it not for the pews they filled
Sundays would come and go
With empty seats and empty church
And God so few would know.

With dress of color and of white
And some that wore a gown
Who bore their burdens of the cross
In time will wear the crown.

LOVE, MERCY:
THE LONG AND SHORT OF IT

by Eugene L. Gable

Love, mercy, truth, and righteousness,
Do good that good will come,
Despise the path of greediness,
From lusting flesh do run.

See good in trials, when trouble comes
Shake not your fist at God
But slowly go and thankful be
You cannot buck the odds.

For time and change are on the way
On wings of morning fly
In healing love of joyfulness
To lift you to the sky.

In time like rain will justice come
And truth unveil the night
Rewards will come to everyone
The evil and the right.

Salvation comes in time of need
For all the good you've done
But woe and grief, and hopelessness
On greedy heads will come.

Accept your struggle in your youth
Though long the time may seem,
For all the pleasures of the world
Will pass as in a dream.

FREEDOM

by Eugene L. Gable

Who cometh here on eagle wings
To break the spell of night
To rob the darkness from the slave
And change our inward night?

The ring that led us by the nose
No longer leads the ox
Our hopes and dreams of things that were
Are dashed upon the rocks.

To find our way where none dost bind
More fearful than the past
From slavery now to find our way
In horror our mind is cast.

Cast not your light upon our mind
In darkness let us be
And show us not the path of life
Of things that make us free.

The evidence of things that are
Was hidden in our youth
To change the way that we perceive
With lies they said were truth.

THE MEASURE OF A MAN

by David L. Gamble

What is the measure of a man?

Do you deal with each man as an individual? Or do you judge him based on some stereotype?

An old black man shuffled across the street, taking his time. Two white men sitting in a pick-up truck remarked, "Just look at the ole lazy black crow draggin' across the street."

You see, all their lives, they had been told that black people are shiftless and lazy. Too bad they didn't get to know this man, who didn't have a lazy bone in his body. A man who could not help the way he walked, for he had a bad back and rheumatoid arthritis in his feet.

A Native American man robs a store, taking money and beer. Then a black woman who witnessed the crime said, "See, they're all just a bunch of drunken thieves." That is what she had been taught all of her life, and here was her proof.

Too bad she never learned about the doctors, teachers, engineers and all around good citizens who were also Native Americans.

The Reverend Dr. Martin Luther King challenged us to judge not based on race, colour, or some stereotype, but on the content of a person's character.

When it comes to people of different races, are you "colour blind"? I implore, yes, I plead with you, TAKE THE BLINDERS OFF. LOOK AT MY BEAUTIFUL COCOA BROWN SKIN. It is a part of who I am. But please don't judge me by it; judge me as an individual.

What is the measure of a man? Look at how he treats his fellow man. Please don't judge him based on the actions of others. For the true measure of a man is in his heart.

MY PRAYER

by David L. Gamble

There was nothing. God looked upon the nothingness, and decided to create a universe.

BOOM!

Suddenly there were particles of matter, clouds of gas and dust, flying in every direction. Then God, in his love and endless wisdom, gently caressed the newly formed matter and spread it out in a pattern across the blackness of space. He swirled it around with his finger to form galaxies.

He rolled balls of many different types of matter all mixed together with his fingers. He made them in various sizes then placed them carefully in an orderly fashion around some of the stars and beautiful planets now moved mightily in their orbits.

He set his sights on one blue planet traveling silently around a bright yellow star. He cleaned away the smoke and dust, and suddenly the sun appeared. And when the planet turned causing its sun to sink below the horizon, then beautiful moon and stars appeared.

Then he pushed the land up from beneath the watery deep. He planted many amazing and breath taking flowers and plants.

He filled the waters with fish and many great creatures. On the land, he artfully created animals, some roamed the land, and others soared through the air.

Then he took a lump of clay, and the Great Potter formed a man. This was his crowning accomplishment on this small planet, for the man was made in his image. Then a deep sleep engulfed the man and God plucked a rib from his side, and formed a beautiful woman. He presented her to the man in all her splendor. This is where we all came from. No matter what skin you find yourself in, no matter the land in which you were born. We all stem from that original pair.

The creator loves us all the same; we are his creation, his children made in his awesome image. My prayer is that we all some day learn to love and care for each other. That every man, woman and child on earth can know that they are truly loved by their fellow humans. That we never forget where we came from. That the Lord God made us all. I pray that we all learn to think of every person that we meet as our brother or sister. For we are all cut from the same cloth.

FOR MY CHILDREN

by Oletha Bostic Gustus

Today I held a hummingbird in the hollow of my hand.
I'd watched it in its fearless, frantic flight from flower to flower,
Sunlight flashing on the iridescent green and gold flecks of its feathers,
Gathering, gathering sweetness, but never taking time to savor.

It flew straight on, pulling up at the last second,
It met with the reality that what appeared to lay ahead
Was simply a reflection of what was behind,
As it crashed against the windowpane.

Stunned it lay, but still alive, one tiny wing askew.
I picked it up and held the weightless warmth in the hollow of my hand.
Gently, gently I aligned its wing,
As it lay pulsating against my palm.

For at least ten minutes I held it there—such a short span
        in the space of a day—
Stroking its head and back, I willed it recovery; willed it to fly again.
As I tried to place it in the red salvia, it felt freedom and lifted from my open palm.
Hovering for a split second, it darted over the rooftop and was gone.

But I had held a hummingbird in the hollow of my hand,
And if I hold my hand just so, and close my eyes, I feel again
        that weightless warmth.

Yesterday I held you against the hollow of my heart, and felt
        your breath against my breast.
It seemed such a short span in the space of a lifetime.
But if I hold my arms just so, I feel you there again,
Heart beating against my heart.

How like that hummingbird your are,
As I watch you now in your fearless, frantic flight from dream to dream,
Sunlight flashing off the glow of your youth,
Gathering, gathering experiences, but taking no time to savor.

I await the day when you too crash against the reality that the future
Is but a reflection of the past.
And things you swore you'd never be, you've now become.
And you'll lie stunned by truth.

Once more I'll hold you against the hollow of my heart, and will you to fly again.
I'll will you acceptance, will you back to balance, and will you to take
        time to savor life's sweetness.

March 26, 1998

SISTER

by Oletha Bostic Gustus

How so alike we were, as I met you there in the Atlanta airport!
I was not looking for you, for we were not siblings separated as infants,
And I had not found you as a result of an exhaustive search of records.
We met solely by happenstance.

There were no familial features to compare.
For our commonality was only that we were daughters of Mother Earth
      and Father God.
I discovered our bond as we faced the blood red sphere of the sunrise
And wondered at its glory.

We spoke of many things,
Of friends, of family, of faith, and how to fix the world.
Our thoughts and ideas were so similar
That I could have talked forever.

But I had a flight to catch, and you had a long row of windows to clean.
And so we took our leave.
I did not ask your name, nor tell you mine,
And that is best, for my memory has named you "**Sister**."

MOTHERLESSONS

By Oletha Bostic Gustus

I walked again with you today
Along mountain paths where dogwood blooms.
We searched once more for those secret places
Where the white violets and wild azaleas grow.

This time, though, there were only the footfall sounds of one
Not three or four as in that other time and on that other mountain.
I know you were there, because when I asked
The whisper of your reply gently rocked the newborn leaves of a sycamore.

Many were the lessons you taught on springtime Sunday afternoons,
"Walk gently, girl. Watch where you step.
Life is fragile, child, and the thoughtless tread from which one
        plant springs back may be fatal to another."
And I know now that applies to people, too.

You taught us to look for beauty in all things and in all places.
We found bright blue 'star-in-the-grass' growing in an old refuse heap;
A 'Jack-in-the-pulpit' by a sulfur-polluted creek;
And the fiddle neck of a fern pushing up from a tiny crack in what
        looked like solid rock.
I look now for beauty in the faces of the human survivors.

The sun went down, and I had to leave you on that quiet mountain.
As I turned to go, my feet stirred the musty layers of summers past
        which nurture the promises of this new spring, and
I could not resist the prayer that this too applies to people
And perhaps those layered lessons learned long ago on springtime
        mountains
Have also been well taught to give hope to another generation.

April 20, 1997
Near Asheville, North Carolina

27

AFTER BEING AT CATALINA STATE PARK

by Betty Henri

Yesterday, I saw birds and
The open sky.
Yesterday I saw the mountains
And brown grass.
And heard the birds.

The birds were lovely, fly-catchers,
All sorts—
The cardinal of brilliant red
And to his lovely Lady,
He sang his song.

Hawks soaring overhead on
Outstretched wings.
The birds on the ground were
Suddenly quiet, no quail calls.
Hawks of different kinds.

Yesterday, I felt the heat of
The sun as it warmed the earth.
Yesterday, I felt the breeze, still
Cool from the winter's blast.
But the earth and I felt the warmth.

Yesterday, I walked up hill and down,
Felt the dirt and rocks under my feet.
Yesterday, I listened to the quiet of
A breeze and songs of birds.
And saw the landscape.

There were small streams, places
For animals and birds to drink and bathe.
Lizards scurried out of the imagined
Enemies' way.
To places dark and hidden.

The very brilliant vermilion fly-catchers
Stationed themselves in full view.
Colors so brilliant,
Painted by the most Imaginative Sophia—
So easily seen.

Yesterday, I saw the contrasting
Towhee and thrashers, hiding.
Darting here and there, with
Shrill calls and chirps.
Not so easily seen.

Tiny, tiny birds, flitting here and
There on branches, feeding,
A jackrabbit bounded out of sight,
Ears standing straight up listening,
Ever wary.

Yesterday, I saw a place where
People lived so long ago.
Yesterday, I saw were they grew
Their food and played games.
A people surviving.

As centuries pass, will someone
Stand on a hill and look
Over the valley and wonder
Who lived there? What did they do?
And why?

As centuries pass, will mountains
And valleys still show silhouettes
Of cactus? Trees? Flowers?
Brown grass?
Will the earth still be—as
Centuries pass?

THREE UNTITLED POEMS

by William Hill

3-3

My poem is lost
I shall never know.

Perhaps it was the one
To cause a change.

But now it is gone
At least I know.

4-5

Remember what you said
About the trees?
Being enveloped in willow branches.
Why, is it because the moon is pale
The night is heavy and warm?
What is it—to be carried away?
Away from oneself,
Alone to care about nothing,
Alone except to feel.

4-7

Got a good thing going,
Going to walk in the sun
Talk to the trees.
Yeah, I'm going to sing in the street.
Don't really know why.
Could be the sun—makes me feel
Good all over.
Sure hope it doesn't rain.
Too cold and uncaring is the rain
Can't jump and shout—for joy.

DRESSED TO BE BLESSED

by Edythe L. Holt

They came to church in a Coupe DeVille
He wore a tailor-made suit, she was dressed to kill.
They walked up the church steps
The usher opened the door
They reminded him of someone who didn't come any more.
He wore a BIG diamond ring, and diamond cuff links too,
On her wrist were many bracelets of gold, all looked new.
Her cape was mink and not very old,
The weather outside wasn't that cold.
The preacher prayed and then he preached,
Some souls he blackened and others he bleached.
It was time for the offering, the choir rose to sing
Everyone in the church who was able,
Walked up to put their money on the table.
The well-dressed couple strutted proudly forth
The preacher looked them over, and judged their worth.
She eased a nickel on the table with her gloved hand
And he plunked down a quarter.
The preacher was so amazed, he choked on a drink of water.

OUR CHILDREN

by Edythe L. Holt

There's one who thinks of Mama,
and brings gifts and flowers.
There's one that thinks of Dad
and wants to borrow the car.
There's one who loves to argue,
to show how smart they are.
There's one who comes to visit,
to talk for hours and hours.
There's one who always listens,
when you give advice about their friends.
There's one who borrows from you,
thinking money never ends.
There's one who calls on the phone,
just to hear your voice.
It's collect, and you accept it,
because you have no choice.
There's one that's very loving,
always greets you with a kiss.
Bring them all together,
It's a time of family bliss.

SOULFOOD REUNION

by Edythe L. Holt

Mustard greens boiled way down
Black-eyed peas and hogshead too
We'll clean the pots till they look like new
Catfish fried to a golden brown

Ham, catfish, and fried chicken
Start lips a-lickin, all eyes over the food are flickin
Brown beans and hocks simmered low
Hot corn bread for the teeth to mow

Yams so tender, juicy, and sweet
All kinds of good vegetables, bread and meat
Makes you stay in the kitchen
Till it's time to eat

Ice cream in the freezer
For old times' sake
Pies, peach cobbler, and dark chocolate cake
Oh, what a feast it all will make

Mama cooked and really got down
The family came from cities and towns
Talked, laughed, prayed, and ate
There was plenty of food for those who came late

All went home
Full up to their chin
Next year we will have
The reunion again

IN LOVE WITH THE SEASONS OF TIME

by Charlene Watson Jones

I'm in love with the seasons of times—
the strong winds that beat against my brow,
the soaking rains that moisten the soil
awaiting a farmer's plow...

With the gentle sunrise in early spring,
and its cool morning breeze,
the warm shimmers of sunlight sifting
softly through undulating trees...

The romance of tiny rosebuds
drenched with fresh morning dew,
fields of sweet smelling wild flowers
in colors of yellow, green, and lavender hue.

I'm in love with the changing winds of autumn
and its various shades of gold, orange and brown,
its swiftness that sends thousands of leaves blowing
with a wanderlust rustling sound...

The warmth and splendor of summer days bright,
and tranquil darkened nights,
the exhilarating stars adorning dusky evening skies
with heavenly lights.

The glow of a full moon orbiting graciously
across a twinkling indigo sky
while sprinkling moonbeams on its way
over wide oceans, rivers, and free running streams.

I'm in love with the chilling frost of winter
that comes at the end of autumn's dawn.
The glistening snow that silently falls
spreading its soft winter blanket
after spring and summer are once more gone.

I'm in love with all the seasons of life,
from the magical joys of childhood
to the challenges and splendors of adulthood.

DO YOU REALLY CARE

by Charlene Watson Jones

If I told you I loved you
would it matter not?
Would you really care?
Would it only merit a phrase to
fill a wordless spot,
or just a romantic venture only
bearing essence to dare?
If I could tell you how much I loved you
in depth or measure,
would it matter not a trite to treasure,
or do you really care
for intimate entities
and times to share?
If I told you I loved you for the
wit and softness of you, for that
special smile that is uniquely yours
and I so very much adore,
would it matter not?
Would you really care?
Knowing all you mean to me
and how much I really care.
With traces of love scattered about
and melodies of troth echoes everywhere,
Still—Does it matter not,
or do you really care?

CRICKET AT MY WINDOW

by Charlene Watson Jones

Flowering shrubbery, palms and evergreens
        shield my bedroom window,
        and yet some invading noisy little creature
        has discovered this secret.

It chirps and chants the same tune night after night
        increasing my anger and regret.
        If only I could find it in the darkness
        and smash it, I would!

Banging on the window and screen to my surprise
        only increases its voice pitch
        in a tone that escapes my recognition
        and tampers with my grit.

Enough of this, I shouted!
        I am going to destroy this aggravating creature
        once and for all!

My fury rose and my anger steamed,
        I opened the curtains and window
        then yanked out the screen.

With a tiny flashlight and armed with a swat,
        I began a deadly search amidst the jungle
        of tree limbs and palm leaves branching out.

Suddenly the noise stopped and behold,
        there it was,
        perched silently on a spindly branch.

Brave, defiant and staunch it stood,
   with all those uninvited noises instilled.
   It was quiet and vain, as though it had
   just finished a performance
   that warranted an encore.

My anger subsided and my fury mellowed at last.
   The chance was mine to smash this cricket at my window.
   And then it would all be over.

My thoughts turned to quiet, peaceful and restful nights
   without this boisterous creature
   awakening me from a peaceful sleep,
   invading my quietness with songs
   of its choice, not mine.

At last I have the chance to put an end to this
   nightly intrusion disrupting my sleep,
   and I will once again drift
   into quiet and peaceful dreamery.

As I raised my hand to finally make that fatal strike,
   within the quick blink of my eyelid, it was gone.
   Darn!
   It had quickly escaped into the darkness
   of the forest of cluttered leaves and shrubbery.

My frustration was in charge and it took its toll.
   Oh, no! I shouted. It got away!

I asked myself, should I pursue this frustrating search?
   Scramble through dead leaves,
   branches with thorns and shrubs?
   Ah, drat!
   I will let the noisy little creature live.

PROPHESY PEACE

by Jeanette Jones

Dream Peace   Bring it into Being

Think Peace   Fill your Heart and Mind with its Essence

Breathe Peace   Send it to every Cell of your God-given body

Whisper Peace   Vibrate the Air in ever widening Circles with its Message

Speak Peace   Spread its Tender Hope and Joy to others in the World

Sing Peace   Tell the People of its Truth and Justice in a rising Crescendo

Dance Peace   Show its Freedom of Movement and Vision for the Future

Play Peace   Let every Child and Adult share in the glorious Game

Prophesy Peace Dream,   To all Coming Generations until They can

Think, Breathe, Whisper, Speak, Sing, Dance, and Play Peace.

May war's endless wounds heal and fade to scars that will never let us forget: war is no way of life.

Remember war WAS NOT part of God's creation.

2003

NESTLED AGAINST HIS KNEES

by Jeanette J. Jones

My prayers are really simple talk
Straight to Him in whose shadow I walk
To Him I pray for things I feel he will give
Simple things like strength, patience, and love to live
And do all that I can and then some
Never too tired, ungracious or glum
To serve a stranger as well as a friend
So that my love for mankind will transcend
The mediocrity of every day.
For these simple virtues I daily pray.
Strength, Patience, and Love from Him whom I would please
For night brings peace and rest nestled against His knees.

MILLENNIUM 2000

by Jeanette J. Jones

Gracious Lord
You have raised up a wondrous people
   Earth People

They shine in their diversity
They glow in their sameness
They give off the aura of Your love.

Their voices are raised in exalted
   praise of You and all that You are.
Their sounds are sweet and loud,
   raucous and sublime.
All emitted in praise of life, love and You.

They rejoice in a myriad of ways.
Their bodies sway and leap to express their joy.
They writhe and bloom to tell of their freedom.

They honor Your Names
They lift up all they are
   to everything You are.

They are all Your cherished children.
They celebrate You!

THE PROPHETS

by Edith Lauver

The teachings of Yahweh fell upon
    deafened ears.
The people sought Baals to allay
    their deep fears.

Throughout Israel and Judah the
    prophets foretell,
"Beware Yahweh's wrath and
    Jerusalem's hell."

Ancient kings ruled, and eventually died;
    some were OK—others incredibly bad;
But, the lessons of God went unlearned,
    oh, how sad!

For the fires burned bright, the skies
    turned to rust.
Many lives were consumed;
    ashes mixing with dust.

From the dust and God's tears,
    a seed sprouted leaf;
A greening of hope amongst
    ashes of grief.

The prophets foretold the future to be.
The birth of the Christ; our Immanuel, he!

MESSAGES FROM MICAH

by Edith Lauver

The earth trembles as ancient cultures collide in battle
between Yahweh's will and that of the Baals.

Yahweh's people cry out from their rulers' oppression;
from those who have led them astray.

Is there no end to the violence and bloodshed?

Read 4:3

"Yes, people," Yahweh says, "When Zion shall hammer its
swords into plowshares and its spears into sickles."

"When each shows love, compassion, and justice
to the lame in one's midst."

Read 6: 6-8

For Yahweh shall gather the lame and the weary
to make a remnant;

And out of this remnant a mighty nation shall be born.

And Yahweh shall reign in peace and love over this nation. Zion,
forever and ever!

Read 5:2-5

Emet and Tzedek,
Hesed and Shalom

WISDOM OF THE SAGES

by Edith Lauver

The collection of Wisdom is confusing, at best;
  no "glue" is apparent, its framework is guessed.

From Proverb's word keys to a life free from sin;
  to Tobit's own story and that of his kin.

Job's heaven on earth and great tribulation;
  we sympathize with his frustrated oblation.

Ecclesiasticus and Ecclesiastes (aka Sirach and
Ooheleth)
  raise questions of faith as we journey toward
death.

Song of Songs depicts feelings on earth and above;
  the Wisdom of Solomon extols Yahweh's love.

The events in these books so swiftly demean;
  God's love and compassion go often unseen.

Wisdom subtly admonishes, then shows us the way;
  We thank you, dear God, for your blessings this
day!

Amen

THE GIFT OF WATER
(FROM O-WAK-SHEE LEGEND)

by Russell P. Long

In the time of The Great Dryness
Then the rivers escaped the heat underground when
Our Brother The Blue Mule Deer ran to The Faraway Mountains
And even Our Brother The Red Rabbit withered
His skin like the face of an old man
The O-Wak-Shee The Desert Dwellers
Danced The Dance of Forgotten Rain and sang The Song of Hunger

Hun-Ta-La-Kow-A Our Father the Great One of the Air and Wind
Led me to The Place between the Stones
Where the water grew like willows and I drank
I drank deeply until my heart swelled with water
And I could drink no more
Then I waited a long time until my thirst returned
And I drank again and filled my parched soul

Hun-Ta-La-Kow-A Our Father bid me
Fill my skins with water and take them
To The Desert Dwellers who cheered and cried and drank
Until the skins were empty and then they placed the cool skins
On their faces and breathed the dryness out of their dusty lungs
Hun-Ta-La-Kow-A then bid me show The Desert Dweller The Place
        between the Stones
Where the water grew and they named it Tuk-A-Shon

They cared for Tuk-A-Shon and made canals for the water to flow out
        to the land
They shared the water with Our Brothers The Blue Mule Deer and
        The Red Rabbit
And gave the water up to Ku-Wah-Tu-Hah Our Mother The Earth
Who raised sweet corn, squash and beans and made the land green again
So The O-Wak-Shee The Desert Dwellers were thirsty and hungry
        no more
They sang and danced and praised the names of Hun-Ta-La-Kow-A Our Father
And of Ku-Wah-Tu-Hah Our Mother The Earth.

2000

THE BAND OF FIVE THOUSAND

by Russell P. Long

On September Eleventh Two Thousand and One
Chicken Little dreamed "The sky is falling, it's come undone."
He rushed outside and there it came
Oboes, violas and French horns it rained.

The Band of Five Thousand were swirling in space
Rising toward heaven Chicken Little rightly knew.
With banners of fuchsia and gold, emerald
The color guard with flags waving red, white and blue.

Captains were issuing orders above
A cacophony of ranks with trumpets ablare.
Divisions of musicians were forming like flocks
And flying as geese in a V through the air.

Sections of firemen led the way to the front
They battled the wind, fought the rain, took the brunt.
Side by side with a chorus of cops, their arms intertwined
Marching to a cadence of drums from on high.

A Jewish Fiddler On The Roof played a sad solo reel
His friend the Muslim with his hand on his shoulder.
The Russian Orthodox bass player saw
That the Fiddler was wounded so he kindly took over.

An Italian Catholic's mandolin was in tune
So he played a duet with an atheist out loud.
The Hindu sitarist was asked to play soon
A hint of curry wafting out through the crowd.

The four postal workers who joined the Band late
Were arranged to perform in a stringed quartet.
The conductor a gay man with baton to direct
Created a song all would never forget.

Below them the onlookers could not believe
That the Band of Five Thousand's song soon would be still.
With smoke and with mirrors they escaped through the clouds
Somewhere Over The Rainbow to a land on a hill.

A wondrous light from whence the musicians had gone
Came showering down on twisted buildings and trees.
The light like white doves brought that most familiar song
Chicken Little in wonder tearfully fell to his knees.

The light flew over the land to all countries on Earth
And to all peoples no matter their race or their worth.
A peace never known and a united flag unfurled
Was a Band of Five Thousand's holy gift to the world.

2002

SOMETHING IN THE FOG
(FOR ROBERT MIRABAL)

by Russell P. Long

There is something in the fog,
A form or a voice—I cannot tell,
It beckons me to curl inside of myself,
Burrow into the snow,
Hibernate in a cave for the winter.

It is from the genes that I am being called,
Ancestral voices in the blood, red and ancient.

Nowhere is it written that
I must think like a human being,
Man with marble chin in hand,
A Grecian statue naked and hard.

I am thinking like an animal at this moment,
Fanged thoughts with curved claws, lethal,
I toy with my prey; bat its softness with my paw.
I feast on fresh meat—it still quivers as I swallow,
Stare from afar at the yellow fires of men,
Throw my head back and howl at the moon.

March 5, 1994

THE CHILD'S HEART

by Sarah Elizabeth Lovinger

They say the best type of gold,
Is found in something that is old.
That touches the heart of many,
And is sure to bring plenty of love and joy
In everyone's heart.
And is found the best
In many parts of the real caring child's heart.

WHAT'S IMPORTANT

by Sarah Elizabeth Lovinger

It does not matter,
If you are spic and span,
No matter what,
You'll always be my superman.
It does not matter,
If you've fought many battles
Or ridden in many saddles,
It matters that you are important in my life.

NIGHTLIGHT

by Sarah Elizabeth Lovinger

It's light, it's bright, it's bold
It's as beautiful as gold,
It's glowing, it's flowing,
It's shimmering in the sun,
It lights up the whole room,
As soon as you turn it on.

Written as a Christmas gift to
Grandparents Richard and Sue Lovinger
Christmas, 2001

I DO NOT UNDERSTAND

by Michael McKenzie

I do not understand
        Why some Palestinian extremists would
        Blow themselves up
        Just to die
        For "their religion"
        Why the Palestinians and Israelis
        Can't agree on something
        Or another
        Why the Palestinian suicide bombings
        And military attacks
        In Israel
        Just won't
        Stop.

But most of all, I do not understand
        Why the "Holy Land" in Israel
        Has to be covered in tanks
        And scorched with the burns
        From the Palestinian suicide bombings
        When things should be
        Peaceful
        (When I watch the news
        I see the Church of the Nativity
        Filled with terrorists
        Surrounded by tanks and soldiers
        While priests and nuns starve).

What I understand most is why people try to get to the U.S.
        Sailing in boats
        Flying in planes
        Risking everything for freedom
        Willing to sacrifice everything for their families.

May 3, 2002

ANGER

by Michael McKenzie

Anger is as dark a as black hole, engulfing all who dare
to come near

It sounds like cat claws, screeching down a chalkboard

It tastes like fire, burning away at the soul

It smells like gasoline, choking me and making me hold
my breath

It looks like a swarm of bees, chasing me away

It scares me and makes me feel sad

MONSOON RAINS

by Matthew Moore

monsoon rains offer
yearly repentance
on this summer Sabbath
as I wander through
the mesquite brush
and hardened saguaros
that offer eternal sanctuary
for our ancestors
I ask your forgiveness
for trespassing my place
amongst these aging souls
planted in your good creation
I confess to you that at times I lost faith
became disheartened with this world
but as I travel on this sacred ground
I ask the rain
to cleanse my spirit
and baptize my soul
to do your will on earth
as I travel these days
I pray to you
always

WHAT'S IN A NAME

by Matt Moore

MATT

M ixed feelings
A rtist
T oo much I must do
T oo much that I can't do

MOORE

M emories that are painful
O utraged at life
O dd ball
R emember things that are bad
E ndurance

Written in 1992 at age 12

STEPPING OUT OF OUR COMFORT ZONE

by Matthew Moore

It is often said "God moves us in mysterious ways."
But I also believe that God moves us in
blatantly obvious, sometimes startling,
but very profound ways.

Most people, at one time in their lives or another,
"wake up" to find themselves being slapped in the face,
grabbed by the shoulders and jarred by God
as she screams right in our face:
"Open your eyes! Do you see me now?
Can you feel my presence now?!
Do you understand my purpose for you?!"

It is at these moments when you come in contact
with the divine presence
in such a physical, personal, and profoundly obvious way
that life, as you knew it, is no longer left the same.

It is, in the deepest sense, a spiritual conversion.
It is at that moment when one is no longer
being politely asked by God to listen to her wishes,
but being sat down and told!

DESERT VEGETATION

by Gloria "Glo" Y. Myers

Dust Devils
are exorcised
by New Life of the soft brown soil.

Wild Flowers
everywhere
Yellow blooms
dancin' with
Orange blooms on
Palo Verde & Ocotillo.

Winds
hot and humid
after the rains
encouragin' life.

Desert vegetations:
flowers, bushes, trees
bloomin', growin'
bowin' in prayer,
thankful for the gentle breeze.

Small blessin' in times of
Huge needs
Pass by unnoticed.

But the new life
on the soft brown soil
seem to bow their heads
bend their knees
Thankful for the blessed gentle breeze.

THE LIFE

by Gloria "Glo" Y. Myers

Lookin' at thangs with a whole new perspective.
sitting here trippin' and I love to trip.

This has been one of those days—so much happens,
chain reaction, action-reaction-action-then...

Reactions
that I'm forced to deal with.
Regardless, collaboration or confrontation,
both are better than no action at all,
Death.

People don't know about death
outside of
going to funerals
dressed in black
cryin'
moanin'
mournin' their loss.

But
there are all kinds of deaths,
at most burials/true funerals
the attendees
laugh, dance, and parrrteee!

The deaths of souls
funerals of minds

where are the mourners now?

At the big table
sippin' wine
nibblin' cheese
gorgin' on delicacies of caviar and pate

where are the mourners now?
on the floor
Dancin'
siknin' slowly
to the melody of the death Waltz
Dirt sprinklin' lightly
beatin' out the rhythm of the funeral dirge

without action there is no reaction without reaction there is death.

ROSE

by Gloria "Glo" Y. Myers

She was a beautiful girl…exceptionally so.

I used to see her on the bus all the time.

Her face was sooo young, delicate, and innocent

A face out of place with her womanly body.

I used to notice the glances/stares she'd receive from men,
Old enough to be her father's father.

I used to be embarrassed for her when she'd blush through her sepia hue,
And become flustered at a loss for answers to calls…propositions
That her young years protected her from fully understanding.

A beautiful flower blooming fast.

A Rose protected by thorns.

Once plucked by insensitive, callous hands.

Beautiful child,

Beautiful flower,

Shrivels…withers…dies.

HUMAN TERMS

by Clyde Phillips III

Earthquakes; mind breaks
Soul shakes; plastic melts
Into a puddle of murky matter.
You have lost control
Over those who have no control
Though still possessing power
Over worlds you've created.

Poster people line your mind
Wasting your time
With the same old line
They ain't for real,
It's crystal clear
Love is a common object
They object to totally.

Love those unable to love
Control, object, or melt in peace
Because you are on human terms.

A POEM ABOUT A POEM

by Clyde Phillips III

I wrote a poem.
It didn't have rhythm or meter.
What it said had meaning
And a whole lot of truth.
Being happy with it
I didn't get phased
By the people reading it,
Until the realization came that they were re-reading
My poem for rhythm
But not getting down to the core.

My poem was becoming plastic
Unable to withstand pressure
Unjelling into a watery mess
Distanced by the nitty gritty.
I wrote a poem
It didn't have rhythm or meter
It had core integrity.

7/8/82

WHAT DO YOU SAY?

by Clyde Phillips III

The darkness covered the wrinkles on his forehead,
Only the noise from the band
Was his alibi for not being able to hear.
Today he was in a state of confusion.
His mind surfaced
His hands started shaking
When he thought about reality.

I search for his lost eyes
Mine also became unfocused.

He told me he loved his people
And that we are beautiful.
But what are we going to do?
We have so much violence.
"I played music for my people
And brought in bands for them to hear.
Now, I'M BROKE AND SCARED OF MUGGERS."

What do I say?
What do I say?

WAITING

by Virginia Selby

I lean my head against the kitchen window
Looking out on a chill January day
Grey dripping skies...weeping silently.
I watch puddles made during the night
Standing on the red patio floor.
Clumps of leaves, tucked into pockets
Around the tree's roots.
Dead, brown tufts of grass
And the empty stare of the children's playhouse windows.
Then my gaze slowly, slowly
Creeps up the tree trunk
Up to its stark and life-less branches
Suddenly I see buds, hundreds of buds,
Hope wrapped in tiny buds,
Patiently waiting...waiting for another spring!

ON GRANDCHILDREN

by Virginia Selby

Somehow…in the years between
Children and grandchildren,
You forget just how loud they can be
First thing in the morning.
You forget they are always hungry
For all the wrong things
And never for what you had planned,
You don't remember all the "stuff"
They come equipped with
And how it spreads out
Encroaching upon every surface
'Til the rooms lose
Any normal appearance.
You have forgotten how many
Clothes they can wear
And then need washing.
You've forgotten how even
The six o'clock news is not
Sacred to them.
You don't remember how easily
They can be BORED.
You adore them and quote them
And would not part with them.
But you have totally forgotten how
Any time, day or night,
Every glass in the house
Is always dirty!

Somehow…you forgot!

THE GUEST ROOM CLOSET

by Virginia Selby

Yesterday's closet was fat
With clothes for vacationing.
Hangers full of denims
For walking along the beach
While waves break silently under your toes.
Warm sweaters for sitting on wharves
Eating lobster, while gulls
Greedily watch for crumbs.
Dresses for church services
In a two-century old white-spired beauty.
A warm robe for early morning coffee
If needed for an extra cozy hug
In a farmhouse kitchen.
Hangers holding casual curl-up-in-a-chair clothes
For book reading or gazing at the river
That meanders past pine trees at lawn's edge.
Beneath the hangers, a row of comfortable shoes
For strolling through museums
Or browsing through antique shops.
Yesterday the closet stood
Stuffed with visitor's clothes.
Now the hangers are lean and lank and bare
Picked clean of two weeks of memories.
Today they are a sorry sight.

A TWENTIETH CENTURY SONNET

by Dr. Paul David Sholin

Boccaccio's *Decameron* is not read much anymore.
      The century he mirrored—a dark cloud.
Black Death came and covered it with a shroud.
      More than half the population was no more.
Survival replaced culture. More in store:
      To question or resent was not allowed.
Crusades and Inquisition: threat of war;
      Both Church and State threw freedom out the door.

Our century too is threatened with a plague.
      Fundamental virus is its source.
Religion and the State give it its force.
      The threat to peace and justice has been made.
Disaster may be freed to run its course.
      Will Hope itself fall victim to this curse?

FOR PEOPLE, LAND, AND DREAM

by Dr. Paul David Sholin

A people washed ashore
From Europe's old debris
With grit, hard work and vigor
Built the colonies.
We saw this world as new;
We risked equality.
Red, white and black brought us their best
And struggled to be free.

The land was here and waiting.
'Twas rugged, rich and wide;
Already blessed with people
Who soon were pushed aside.
From East to West we settled.
We trailed and tilled the sod.
We were not always faithful
Have mercy on us, God!

The dream made us a people—
Self-government and more.
We lighted fires of freedom
Seen far beyond the shore.
Two hundred years we've weathered;
Been tested, tried, refined.
The dream is still worth living
For the sake of humankind.

For people, land and dream
We offer thanks this day.
For heritage and hope,
And freedom when we pray.
We hunger for the time
When our dark shadows flee.
When all we have and hope to be
Help shape Earth's family.

July 4, 1976
(received a State-wide prize in 1976)

SAINT PATRICK (385 – 461)

by Dr. Paul David Sholin

Legend is the source for what we know
Of Patrick, now the Patron and the toast
Of Old Ireland of whom they boast.
This missionary monk, it can be shown,
Brought faith and hope and love to those
Who enslaved him as a child off Britain's coast.
We used the shamrock's triple leaves of green
To talk of God, Creator, Christ and Holy Ghost.

Pope Leo in four hundred forty-four
Made Patrick the Archbishop of Armagh.
He rid the Isle of snakes and banished fear;
Preserving learning in the place of lore.
This Saint deserves our honor and our awe,
A man that millions hold dear.

PUSHING YEARS YOUNG

by David Thompson

Pushing years young
After pulling years old
My great grandmother is toughing it out
Putting her round wreath where we try to wonder
Hoping she raises her eyes to see it.
Possessing her jaunty girlhood yearnings,
She wanders in reach of old memories.
Poking her rings and grieving for lost love,
Always pleasure in her eyes,
My lovely great grandmother keeps time.
I listen to her stories, and the stories we all tell about her.

Pushing years young
After pulling years old
My great grandmother is learning it still.
Joking this noon from politics in the news
She reaches right into the midst.
Laughing with long cheers she rings out the truth
Juggling her past with the present.

Pushing years young
After pulling years old
My great grandmother wants knowledge yet.
Listening more carefully we long to go into her hopes
All of us flock to sit by her side.
Will her world be diplomatic and proper
Or likely like ours, lost in sex and loud words?
She goes through it watching and learning.
She asks how we look at the world,
She asks what we wonder about.
She knows what growing up is,
She understands old.

Pushing years young
After pulling years old
My great grandmother is yearning for hope.
Her grandchildren grown have children in years
Her great grandchildren live this life
Her best victories are past
Her world is here and then.
She touches our lives in truth understanding this is just in the present.

Pushing years young
After pulling years old
My great grandmother holds onto her life.
Each day is like many
Up past the dawn and asleep in the day,
She tries to live each moment.
Looking out under roof under windshield
She watches the palms and playing birds.
Hours are yours, minutes are hers.

Pushing years young
After pulling years old
My great grandmother basks in the daylight
Treasuring the past and opening her soul to love.

TASTE LIFE WITH ME

by David Thompson

See into my eyes
Look high in the sky
Another task for hope

Touch my anger
Search the day
Take your time in this

Taste my pure feelings
Pass over the clouds
Push the fears away

Feel my love for friends
Find your great hope
Go with me in your dreams.

Written at age 12

THE MOON

by David Thompson

The moon is a big silver balloon
That pops across the night sky.
Where does the helium go when the moon sets?

The moon is music.
It sings slowly through the night.
Why does the music fade?

The moon is a desert.
Its stillness calms my racing heart.
Does it calm another's heart?

The moon is the measure of time.
It counts each night for eternity.
But how much time is really left?

The moon is a wolf's delight.
They howl to it from dusk till light.
Which wolf will howl tonight?

WOODSMOKE

by Annelle Warren

My pulse quickened by a fragrance on the wind:
The smell of woodsmoke in the afterglow;
I walk the blue enchanted way again tonight,
The path we came so very long ago.

The scattered leaves are scuffed by other feet than mine:
I know I walk companioned by a ghost—
When woodsmoke on the autumn air is sharply blown
I know how far away you are, and I—how lost.

LEGACY
FOR J. AND C.

by Annelle Warren

Little I have to leave to you:
a quickened eye for loveliness,
a coin of humor quickly spent,
the ghost of had-I-loved-you-less;
no concrete gifts like bicycles,
no heritage of curly hair—
only the wonder of a heart
half mystic, half aware.
I give you roads I walked upon
and skies I left unspanned,
knowing you have the means to hold
all magic in your hand.

NOW ANOTHER APRIL

by Annelle Warren

The sunlight lies in gleaming strips
Across the pale, parched grass.
Flamboyantly the scornful winds
Proclaim the way they pass.

But in my mind the day is deep
In shadow, and the line
Between the earth and sky is drawn
Particularly fine.

I should not care if roofs must leak
If on my ears could fall
A sound that is so fresh and faint
It's scarcely sound at all.

I should not mind my muddy boots
If I could walk again
Into the fragrant April air,
Communicant of rain.

THE DEEP END

by Chloe Wright

He was a child of the ocean
But had never seen the sea
He was the son of a linguist
But silent always was he
His mother, she despised the dirt
But he grew in it with care
And raised the little green things
That poked up their leaves for air

He was quiet, silent, placid
Just still, all the time
But behind his eyes, those wandering eyes
Thoughts strayed, meandered,
were born and had died
In the space inside his mind

He was brilliant, bright, genius-like,
In his taciturn way,
And his bright blue eyes would flash and light
With every thought that he would say

It was a plain, plain shell he wore
Like the off-white of an egg
That blends in so utterly
With a thousand other eggs

But he was like a light in the darkness
A lily amongst the tawdry plain
Brilliant would he ever gleam,
Against the backdrop of the mundane

And no one else could see it,
No one else would hear
But the brilliance that I saw within
I'll treasure ever dear

And now, so now,
When many years have we all gained
I listen in bitter melancholy
As to his brilliance others lay claim
But I always tried to listen
And I think I understood
And I think he really meant it
When he gave up on childhood

And I think I finally get it,
I think I understand
Why he embraced me warmly,
And held onto my hand

He said, "You're always on my mind,
And first inside my heart
You're here in a special place
And never will we part."

I wanted to hold onto him
And never let him know
That deep, deep down inside,
I knew I had to let him go

He was a child of the ocean
But he never saw the sea
He was the son of a linguist
But he only spoke to me

His bright blue eyes would never more
Flash with thought or word
And when they laid him down,
I was the only one who heard

His mother she despised the dirt,
But there he made his bed
And I tucked in all the li'l green things
To lay there at his head

I had smiled when they lowered him,
Laughed helpless, through my tears
Because happier would he be there,
Than what he'd be upon this sphere

And now, as I sit here with my departed friend,
Only one thought strikes me deep;
He was a child of the ocean,

But he had never, ever seen the sea.

MEDLEY

by Jessie Zander

Lovingly you came
Supplementing life's journey
Non-orchestrated.

Such intrusion
Into lives well formed
Requires assimilation.

Recognition came
Suddenly, between moments
Totally unexpected.

We touched Spirit
Through gentle, probing talk
Signaling reconnection.

I trusted your lead
Some kind of mind expansion
Truth was my bridge to you.

A faith force guides the path
Connects my intuition
To effortless courage

Tapped a reservoir
Reached an emotional place
With deep tangled roots.

Distance gives us time
To absorb, assimilate
This gift of friendship.

So, what is love
A drink of bubbling friendship
Distilled and purified?

Lovingly you stay
Transforming my journey
Unraveling containment.

DISCERNMENT

by Jessie Zander

Dear God,

I got some nerve, huh?
Bending your ear when you have so much
Stuff to do,
People to listen to and problems to solve.
Since I'm one of your children, too, though
I have a right to ask you—
What do you plan to do
About the Mother Country, Africa?
You done abandon her and that's not right.
She been fighting a long time
Tossed and turned and
Shaped into an image of fluidity
Now poisoned with the
Threat of annihilation.

What you gon' do 'bout Africa's Children?
Her blood seeps in the ground
Flows down the river Nile
Settles on the bottom of the Atlantic
Runs through the veins of the peoples of the world.
Will she vanish like Egypt
And her descendents with her?

Now, I know you have the power
You must be choosing to hold that
Awesome power of yours.

Are you passing the question on to France, Germany,
Switzerland, England, Los Angeles, Kansas, Texas, Tucson?
If you have, then your grand plan
Is really well hidden.

Could you be doing that reversal again
Throwing the question back?
We ain't ready to answer you yet, Lord.

A-men, Jessie

Dear Jessie,

Aren't you a bit picky?
Sure, Africa is transforming,
But you didn't mention Ireland, Israel, Russia, or Bosnia.
Are they not in transformation as well?
Their blood flows mingled down.
Their children cry and yearn.

Your question is too narrow
You are right.
The question is for the peoples of the earth.
It should be:
What are we going to do
About the earth's children?
They are fat, less educated and
Equipped for jobs and loosing their core
While you Slogan about the 21st Century. Indeed!

My suggestion to you, Jessie
Is that you look the situation over
Carve the part you can handle
    Handle it
      Carefully
        Consistently
          Lovingly in conjunction
With anyone currently in the caring mood and go to work
Extend your work
Until it approaches satisfaction.

              God

THE UNIFYING SYMBOL

by Jessie Zander

Hey there,
    You
        With the extensions,
            those dangling four
            and the five varied holes in one,
There—
            as Center
            of the all-encompassing space.
            I'd like to join you
            In a trip toward healing,
            Toward harmony and wholeness.
Hey there,
    You
        With the solid part
the protrusions
the extra fuzzy softness
            There—
            as all-encompassing space
            with a Center
            I invite you to join me
            In a swing toward awareness
            Toward change and freedom.
Hey there,
    You
        With the power to create;
            Fantasy to reality
            Reality transformed
        There—
            as a link to my center
            we can enjoy a wider space
            Say the word and I'll join you
            In a walk toward exchange
            Toward a new consciousness and
            understanding.

Hey there!

ABOUT THE AUTHORS

Gladys M. Ahmad (Prince Chapel AME) was born in Patterson, Louisiana. She received a B.A. from Southern University, Baton Rouge, Louisiana. Her postgraduate work was as a reading specialist at the University of Arizona. She has worked as an elementary and middle school teacher for over thirty-three years, twenty-seven of which were in the Tucson Unified School District. She is a storyteller of African folk tales and has written over twenty-five poems and prayers. She is the mother of three and the grandmother of four.

Rachel Campbell (St. Mark's Presbyterian Church) The poems submitted by Rachel were written when she was a middle school student at St. Gregory College Preparatory School where she was a member of the Poetry Club. Rachel loves writing free verse on day-to-day aspects of every teenager's life. She has had poetry published in her school's literary magazine and other school publications.

Louise "Lou" Carter (St. Mark's Presbyterian Church) Lou was born in Dallas, TX in 1918. She had a thirty-one year career in Civil Service working with the U.S. Air Force in St. Louis, Washington, D.C. and Virginia. Lou wrote many poems and had a small volume of her work printed for her friends. She passed away on February 27, 2003.

Laona J. Crutcher (Prince Chapel AME) was born in Chicago, Illinois where she was educated and lived until 1998 when she moved to Tucson, Arizona. Laona received a Master of Christian Education degree from UFBL, and majored in Voice at Wilson Junior College and the Chicago Conservatory of Music. She sings with the Tucson Arizona Mass Choir.

Leticia Fagg (St. Mark's Presbyterian Church) was born in Queensland, Australia where she grew up and obtained her teaching degree. She now resides in Tucson, Arizona where she lives with her husband and three daughters. Leticia teaches four and five-year-olds at St Mark's Preschool and Kindergarten.

Brenda A. Fleming (Prince Chapel AME) was born in Mobile, Alabama and raised in Columbus, Ohio. After graduating from high school she continued her education and graduated from Ohio State University, receiving a Bachelor's degree in Art Education. While a student at Ohio State University, Brenda completed her first book of poetry. This book included one of her first poems written in 1974, "Black Child, Why Do You Cry?" Brenda has been a member of the Armed Forces since 1979, when she joined the Ohio Army National Guard. She later transferred to the Ohio Air National Guard. During this time she also worked full-time as a Franklin County Deputy Sheriff. In 1991 Brenda got the opportunity to serve on active duty as a military training instructor, and in 1996 she was able to enter active duty permanently. She currently works as a Military Equal Opportunity Advisor for the Air Force and is stationed at Aviano, Italy. Brenda continues to enjoy writing and sharing her poetry with others.

Eugene Gable (Prince Chapel AME) was born and raised in Billings, Montana. He spent four years in the Navy. In 1968 he moved to Tucson, Arizona where he met his second wife. They were married in 1977 and have been happily married for twenty-five years. Eugene is the father of three sons, a daughter and four step-daughters. He has fourteen grandchildren and one great grandchild. Eugene retired from the University of Arizona where he was employed for over twenty-five years. He currently works part-time at Prince Chapel.

David L. Gamble (Prince Chapel AME) is a freelance writer who grew up in New Haven, Connecticut. He received a B.S. in Applied Computer Science from Yale University. His poems have appeared in the *New Haven Advocate* and the *Catalina Mail Express*. His work in the computer industry ranges from networking to web design. He is also an actor, comedian and public speaker.

Oletha "Lee" Bostic Gustus (St. Mark's Presbyterian Church) was raised in West Virginia. After attending Fairmont State College for two years, she transferred to the University of Arizona where she earned a B.S. in 1959 and M. Ed.'s in 1969 and 1986. She is retired after forty years as a teacher and counselor. Writing is one of her hobbies, along with volunteer work and singing with the Tucson Arizona Mass Gospel Choir. She is the mother of three children.

Betty M. Henri (St. Mark's Presbyterian Church) was born in Fort Collins, Colorado. She was married in Oregon and started her family there. She returned to Colorado where she found herself writing and delivering sermons once or twice a year. Eventually she took classes in a small community college, and in a Creative Writing class she learned to give her imagination rein. With imagination on the loose, some poetry and a story developed.

William "Bill" Hill, Jr., (Prince Chapel AME) was born in Alexandria, Louisiana and grew up in Tucson, Arizona. He attended the University of Arizona and served in the United States Navy during the Vietnam War. After being discharged from the Navy, Willie settled in San Francisco, California where at various time he sold business forms, office machines and pharmaceuticals for a living—and wrote short stories and poetry for his passion. Several of his works were published in magazines. Willie loved books, reading and the written word in every form, from poetry to novels. His love of books led him to Houghton Mifflin Publishing Co. and Denver, Colorado in the 1970's. As a sales representative for the company, his territory included the Western United States. He moved to Seattle in 1979, continuing to represent Houghton Mifflin in the Northwest. He took an early retirement from the company in

1998. In 1999, he launched AfriCarib Ltd., an Internet business offering museum-quality art from Africa and the Caribbean Islands. He died unexpectedly in Seattle, in May 2000. His sister, Dr. Lorraine Hill Richardson, offers his poems for this work.

Edythe Holt (Prince Chapel AME) describes herself as a retired Grandmother. After her marriage, while being a homemaker and mother of four, she returned to school and entered the Business College at Burlington, Iowa. Upon finishing college she became secretary at the junior high school that three of her children were attending (the same school that she had attended). There she started writing poems and stories for children and enrolled in a correspondence course for writers. Currently she constructs word puzzles and crafts for children's magazines, and also writes and has published poems. Her crafts and puzzles have been published in *Lollipops, You, Highlights, Crayola Kids*, and *Good Apple Magazine*. She keeps active, visiting schools and day care facilities to read poems to the students.

Charlene Jones (Prince Chapel AME) is a writer and poet. Her poems have appeared in *Our World's Most Cherished Poems, World of Poetry* and *American Poetry* anthology. She recently published a children's book, Lobster Kids. Her formal education includes liberal studies at Langston University and religious education at Oklahoma School of Religion. She has an Associate Degree in general studies and health management from Pima Community College.

Jeanette J. Jones (St. Mark's Presbyterian Church) was born in White Plains, New York and came to the University of Arizona in 1951. There she has earned degrees as a Bachelor of Fine Arts, Master of Education for grades K-12, and Master of Education in the field of emotionally handicapped children. She worked ten years in the Art Department at Hughes Aircraft and then for twenty-six years taught emotionally handicapped children in the Tucson Unified School District. She married native Tucsonan Don D. Jones and raised one daughter, Joanna. Jeanette is a voracious reader and enjoys writing her thoughts in poetry.

Russell P. Long (St. Mark's Presbyterian Church) is a 1967 graduate of Tucson's Catalina High School and a 1973 graduate of the University of Arizona. He has a B.A. in English Literature and Writing with emphasis on poetry writing. After graduating from the U of A, he taught English and Speech and was the Speech and Debate Coach at Tucson's Cholla High School from 1973-1977. Since 1977 he has been working for the family business, Long Realty Company, as a salesman, manager and vice president. He lives in Tucson with his wife Christy and their dogs Cozette and Winston, and has two daughters who are involved with the arts. He believes the finest poetry moves through the brain to the pen as a gift that needs little or no revision.

Sarah Lovinger (St. Mark's Presbyterian Church) is the grandchild of St. Mark's member Sue Lovinger and resides in Hillsdale, Michigan where she attends Will Carlton Academy as a fifth-grader. Her poems have been published in *A Celebration of Young Poets—Michigan* in 2000, 2001 and 2002. Sarah enjoys ballet, piano, soccer and reading. She loves to travel, and especially enjoys visiting her grandparents in Tucson.

Edith Barbour Lauver (St. Mark's Presbyterian Church) was born and raised in North Tarrytown, New York. She received a B.S. in Nursing from Skidmore College, an M.A. from Columbia University, and completed the academic program for the Ph.D. degree at the University of Arizona. She has lived in Tucson, Arizona since 1960, and she and her husband are the parents of three sons and grandparents of two granddaughters. She has held a variety of professional nursing positions and currently serves as Director of the Interfaith Coalition for the Homeless. She has authored professional nursing articles, poetry for her friends, and is working on a biography of her great grandfather's Civil War experiences. She is a member of the Society of Southwestern Authors.

Michael McKenzie (St. Mark's Presbyterian Church) is a freshman at Tucson High School. He plays saxophone in the school band and several other jazz groups. He plans to pursue a career in marine biology and/or music.

Matthew Moore (St. Mark's Presbyterian Church) was a talented and loved young man who died of a heart attack on May 31, 2003 at the age of 23. Matt was born with a congenital heart defect and survived six open-heart surgeries throughout his life. He maintained a love of life, and served his God and fellow travelers along life's journey. Matthew was impassioned to help those in need, be it homeless folks or migrants in the desert, and traveling on peace missions to foreign lands. He loved the desert; the monsoon rains, the landscape, the people and the challenges of such a harsh yet beautiful environment.

Matt was the youth director at St. Mark's Presbyterian Church. Completing his early education in the Tucson Unified School District's Magnet School Program, he was finishing his degree in Liberal Arts at the University of Arizona. He was a social activist and was involved in many community organizations throughout his life.

Gloria Yvonne Myers (Prince Chapel AME) was born in the basement of the St. Joseph's Hospital in Fort Worth, Texas in 1954. She moved to Tucson, Arizona with her parents Norma and Morris; sisters Phyllis, Mozelle and Mary, and brother Eddie. Brother Morris Jr. was born in Tucson two years later. Gloria earned her Bachelor of Fine Arts degree with emphasis on Theater Production from the University of Arizona in 1978. She founded the Nkyimkyim Story Theater in 1980 and has worked as a professional storyteller since 1979. Presently Gloria is an Instructional Technician/Academic Specialist with the African American Studies Department of the Tucson Unified School District. She is the mother of two children, Bryana and Conley, and grandmother of Avontae. Her sister Phyllis is a member of Prince Chapel AME.

Clyde Humphrey Phillips III (St. Mark's Presbyterian Church) was born in 1952 in Wichita, Kansas, the second child of Amanda and Clyde Phillips II, both members of St. Mark's. Clyde lived a life of resistance to the invalid world dictated by his health condition. As an infant, he had rheumatic fever and developed epilepsy as a teenager. He went on to graduate from Wichita

Heights High School. He attended Friends University and graduated from Lincoln University (Missouri) in 1975. He worked as a counselor in corrections, mental health, and drug programs in Arizona and Missouri. He was last employed by Central Kansas City Mental Health service. Through understanding he reached out to others, valuing the human experience in word and deed. He wrestled with learning his place in the world by writing eloquently of an individual struggle to manhood. His work has universal appeal. It has "core integrity." Clyde Phillips passed away in March 1995, leaving his wife, Sherrie and son, Robbie. His mother, Amanda Phillips, submitted his work.

Virginia B. Selby (St. Mark's Presbyterian Church) was born in Corinth, Mississippi, the only child of a large extended family. After completing her college degree, she moved to New York City where she worked in marketing research. Marriage brought her to Tucson where the birth of two children completed her family. At a very early age, Virginia says she "started writing poetry that was badly spelled and even worse in rhyme." In recent years while taking a writing course, she has enjoyed writing poetry again and is also writing her memoirs for her children and grandchildren.

Paul David Sholin (Pastor Emeritus St. Mark's Presbyterian Church) is a Presbyterian minister. He graduated from Princeton Seminary and did graduate work at the University of Arizona. He was the organizing Pastor of St. Mark's Presbyterian Church where he served for thirty-eight years, retiring in 1984. As a social activist he worked in the national church and in Arizona, Mexico, and Central and South America. He still resides in Tucson with his wife Norma and German Shepherd Brunner.

David Thompson (St. Mark's Presbyterian Church) was born in Providence, Rhode Island in 1984. He graduated from high school in Boulder, Colorado in 2003 and will begin studying for his major in English literature at the University of Colorado/Denver this fall. David does not speak, but uses Facilitated Communication to communicate. He writes:

"What Facilitated Communication looks like is different for each person, but it requires one person to facilitate the typing of a person who can't talk. The facilitator holds the person's hand or arm, but never does the typing for the person who can't talk. Facilitated Communication is a way for people who can't speak to communicate with their hands.

"Life before FC was difficult. I felt frustrated most of the time. Very few people knew how I felt and no one could tell that I was very smart and learning all the time. When I was in first grade I made friends, but I was very misunderstood. We lived in Louisville then, and my friends learned that I was a kid just like them. I was very glad to go to school in my neighborhood. When I lived in Lakewood I had gone to awful schools for kids with disabilities, and I was miserable. When my teachers and parents found out about Facilitated Communication I felt hope that I could be understood. Instead of getting my desired friends I had my friends in name only. What I wanted then and now were friends who felt comfortable typing with me and asking me to do things with them. Each year I had friends, even if they couldn't be fully my friends. Since I started going to Shining Mountain Waldorf School I have some of the best friends I've ever had.

"Until I went to meet Stephen Hawking I didn't know that I was part of a group of people who used technology in order to communicate. He wanted us to phase in as spokespeople for people who need science to quite quickly make devices we need. Since then I have known that I have an important part to play as a well-educated and interested person. What I think I might be able to do is to learn more about people who use technology to communicate and tell as many people as possible what we need.

"I am really pleased to be in Shining Mountain Waldorf School. With just people and very many opportunities for learning about myself and the world, I have begun to feel optimistic about the future. Since tenth grade I have worked with my good friend and facilitator to become much more independent. We are great at Facilitated Communication. I have been in a group of very loving friends and teachers who give me hope and encouragement. We are going to end this high school life by going to New York City. I decided to raise money for the trip by doing a hike-a-thon, and my friends have decided to join me in hiking the fifty miles. Having friends is the most important thing in life. With the friends I have made at SMWS I know whatever happens after school I am going to get friends wherever I find myself."

David is the grandson of Charles and Jean Ares of St. Mark's.

Annelle Warren 1911-1990 (St. Mark's Presbyterian Church) Annelle's early poems were widely published and were included in three anthologies. Her humor, keen insight, and razor-sharp observation is evident in her many poems. Annelle was a member of St. Mark's for forty years, sang in the choir, and was a member of the Session. Her husband published a special edition of her writings about the Scriptures in 1995 especially for members of St. Mark's. The poems included in this book were the first ones submitted when the idea for this publication was still a dream.

Chloe Wright (Prince Chapel AME) currently attends Northern Virginia Community College and majors in illustration. She does part-time work building and designing WebPages and doing marketing consultation for small businesses. Her poems, essays and photographs have been published in the annual *Cadence Anthology* as well as school magazines and publications. Chloe is the granddaughter of Charlene Watson Jones.

Jessie Zander (St. Mark's Presbyterian Church) was a teacher, counselor, principal, and consultant with the Tucson Unified School District for thirty years. She received a B.A. from Berea College, a double M.A. in Education and Counseling, and an Administrative Certification from the University of Arizona. She is a member of the Arizona State Poetry Society. Her poems have appeared in the Tucson chapbook *Brush the Mind Gently*, 1984; the *Tucson Sun Press*, 1995; and the *Appalachian Independent*, her hometown paper. In 1980, the Far Western Region of Alpha Kappa Alpha Sorority awarded Jessie the Certificate of Merit for selections from her unpublished manuscripts *Slices of Life* and *Threads in the Fabric*.

INDEX OF THE POETS AND POEMS

Printed in the United States
19076LVS00006B/289-390

9 781587 363115